A SHORT STORY ABOUT

EVE:

IT WAS NOT AN

APPLE

(MYSTERY SOLVED)

D1280193

VERA SQUIRE

A SHORT STORY

ABOUT EVE:

IT WAS NOT AN

APPLE

(MYSTERY SOLVED)

<u>INTRODUCTION</u>

Before I can speak about EVE, I must first speak about ADAM.

But before I can speak about ADAM, I must first speak about GOD.

Although the subject of EVE is widely spread in many religions and their subject matter, I have chosen to state the facts from the King James Version of the Bible, and a few of my own views, on EVE.

GOD

THE CREATOR

It was, in the beginning, God. He looked into nothing and created something, just by speaking the words, "Let there be light. And it was, and it was good."

Because God is great, and God is good. His greatness comes from His grace, His mercy, and His love.

He is magnificent and omnipresent (Ever Present.)

And He is Omnipotent (Almighty.)

<u>(Read Gen. Chapter 1, it states the facts).</u>

When you read the Bible, it soon becomes clear to you.

When you take a closer look at this self-explanatory form of collective ways the Creator created this world, you can see the magnitude of His power and love.

Because it was out of His love, He created this world. Before I continue, I would like to take a closer look at this analysis, and comment upon its findings.

You see, God created this world in 6 days, and on the 7th day, God rested.

Now to continue, God is God, and beside Him there is no other.

Even today when you look at the universe through a telescope, you can plainly see the vast array of constellations taking place in a war of worlds' that seems worlds apart.

Now to speak about Adam.

<u>ADAM</u>

Everything was coming up roses in the Garden of Eden, and everything was in its proper place.

Every animal as well as everything that flew and every plant that grew, they were all about their daily routine.

Everything was completed except the making of man.

Now when Adam came on the scene it was noted in,

<u>(Read Gen. 2:7, it states the facts).</u>

I can just imagine how God made the man. The work must have begun from the ground up. It's a mind-boggling situation as you can very well imagine. But with God all things are possible.

On that day, the wind probably was not blowing, and the air must have been as still as the night, but the work went on as planned.

Now the particles from the dust of the ground were formed to make the man.

THE MAKING OF MAN

The head bone was connected, as well as the neck bone, and every component of the anatomy of making of man was prepared to form this clay from the dust of the ground.

The last thing God did to complete this process of making man was to breathe into his nostrils the breath of life, and man became a living soul.

You see, every word God spoke, God breathed. And every time God breathed, He breathed life.

MAN:

IN THE GARDEN OF EDEN

This day was like no other day when God placed man in the Garden of Eden. The man stood tall above the rest. (not above God).

But the things He would give man dominion over.

God specifically gave man authority over everything, but there was also one thing God gave the man and that one thing was a command.

(Read Gen. 2:15-17, it states the facts).

Now Adam went on his daily routine naming all the animals and every fowl of the air, and so on…as God instructed him to do.

God looked around and saw there was not anyone suitable for the man. God said, "it is not good for man to be alone. I will make him a help mate for him."

The Lord God caused the man to fall into a deep sleep and while he was sleeping, he took one of Adam's ribs and closed the place with flesh.

(Read Gen. 2:18-21, it states the facts).

As Adam awoke from his sound anatomy, he saw the operation was a complete success. When Adam stood up, he saw a wonder.

God presented him with this wonder. He must have stared into her eyes and began to say these words.

Adam said, "You are bones of my bones and flesh of my flesh. You shall be called Woman because you were taken out of Man."

(Read Gen. 2:22-23, it states the facts).

After the dust had settled the wind was still and silence remained golden, to this groom and his bride, as they walked side by side, and hand in hand. Soon they took one giant leap into a world of uncertainty on their wedding day.

I can just imagine Adam saying these words to Eve as he looked into her eyes.

Bones of my bones, and flesh of my flesh, the wind that fills the air we breathe, with each breath we take to consummate this oneness.

Bones of my bones and flesh of my flesh. From my side, God weaved you.

From my rib, God formed you.

With every step we take, we take together.

Although, sometimes apart, but not in heart, as we live in Paradise forever.

Then Eve responded to Adam by saying these words.

As I look upon you from head to toe; as you sweep me off my feet, I exhale.

I am the gift God presented to you, and in return, you are my reward.

Now the Bible states: Adam said to the woman, "Your name shall be called Eve."

Eve means the mother of all living.

(Read Gen. 3:20, it states the facts).

EVE

THE MOTHER OF ALL NATIONS

Youth defines Eve. Beauty defines her best, as she finds
her way in life.

She was still in her fragile stage feeling her way as
she walked through, The Garden of Eden.

Eve's complacency sometimes changed her complexion
on life as she stood in a world of completion.

Her task would not be as easy a journey as she thought. You see, I could just imagine, Eve was still in her fragile stage of life, while she was walking through this journey called Paradise.

Her husband Adam was by her side as they walked through the nudity in life. But their serenity world would soon be disrupted by a slurring serpent called the devil.

The dark cloud was beginning to come across the clear sky in their lives as the devil approached them. Soon Eve would find herself in a one-on-one conversation with the serpent, and it would change their lives forever.

EVE

THE CONVERSATION

(Read Gen. 3: 1-6, it states the facts).

You will find out, soon Eve was open to this deceit.

THE FALLING APART

It would not be long before Eve's curiosity had got the best of her because the serpent tricked Eve into biting The Forbidden Fruit.

Eve took The Forbidden Fruit off the tree and bit from it. After she bit the fruit, she immediately gave the fruit to Adam to take a bite, and he did.

The Bible states when Adam bit from the fruit their eyes were open, and they knew they were naked, and they went and hid.

Because that day, their eyes were not just open to Paradise, it was open to the world.

(Read Gen. 3:7, it states the facts).

Banish from Eden

(Read Gen. 3:8-24, it states the facts).

EVE

Eve: The Apple

Before I continue with the story of Eve, I would like to tell you about The Apple.

Let me start by saying why I said, "it was not an apple."

Let me start from the beginning.

When I was writing the story of Eve, I had a dream about, "The Forbidden Fruit."

Well, it was on a clear day in the year 2007, when I had this dream.

Now this dream was a kind of dream one would have when you might drift off to sleep, or when you take a quick snooze.

I would like to describe this dream for a moment. I saw a hand reaching for the fruit on a tree. The hand was of a Biblical statue. Well, I knew then, in my dream, I was not in America.

This remarkable event taking place before my eyes was frightening.

Let me explain.

The hand that reached for the fruit was quite hesitant for a moment, but it soon took the fruit off the tree.

In fact, in my dream, I felt like I was looking at "The Forbidden Fruit" from the book of Genesis.

This remarkable event would soon solidify my inclination of my present thought. Is this,

"The Forbidden Fruit?"

THE FRUIT

THE ANSWER

The fruit looked to be a tropical fruit with many seeds.

To me, the fruit reflected the mold of humanity. It was just like the many nations of people multiplying to flourish the earth, according to the word of God.

My curious nature wanted to explore a little deeper on this subject matter.

I continue to do some research about this fruit, and this is what I found out.

I found out that in almost every religion this fruit has been used as a symbol of human belief and desires.

It also symbolizes Life, Death, Eternal Life, Fertility, Marriage, Abundance and Prosperity.

This fruit looked like a "POMEGRANATE."

The Jews: They believe this fruit represents righteousness and the Jews also believe this fruit was "The Forbidden Fruit."

The Christians: They believe this fruit represents life and hope for eternal life.

The Chinese: They believe this fruit represents wealth and many sons.

JUST FOR THE RECORD

Wait, let me clarify myself on this subject matter, "The Pomegranate and the dream behind it."

Before I started researching on the fruit, I had no recollection of any religious beliefs of any kind about this fruit.

When I had this dream, it was spontaneously, shown to me in a quick flash when I was writing the story of Eve as I nodded off to sleep.

There is no other way I can possibly explain myself.

When I decided to complete the story of Eve, I wanted to include the dream behind it.

There you have it, some facts about

"The Pomegranate" and the weight that it carries throughout time and throughout generations.

Now to continue the story of Eve.

THEIR NEW WORLD

Soon Adam and Eve began a family. Adam knew his wife, Eve, and she conceived a child and his name was Cain. Then Eve soon had another child, because the Bible states that Adam knew his wife Eve again, and she conceived another child and his name was Abel.

(Read Gen. 4:1-2, it states the facts).

It wouldn't be long until their strength would be tested.

You see, their second child was murdered by their first child, and that must have been a heavy burden for them to carry.

I could imagine how Adam and Eve were. They must have been devastated by this tragedy.

Eve had to stand tall as her counterpart did. Adam began to lift Eve off the ground as she grieved.

Because they knew nothing about death, only life.

While Adam comforted Eve, he began to say these words.

"One voice, one sound, one whisper, is a moment we have in life. Breathe while we can, the breath that was given to us by God. Because each breath of life is a gift from God and each moment is precious."

Eve responded to Adam by saying,

"This moment we share is captive in time, and so is the love we have for our child Abel, who is captive in our heart."

The Bible states that Adam knew his wife Eve again, and Eve soon was with another child and his name was Seth. When Seth was born and grew up to be a man, Seth knew his wife and their first child was named Enos.

Now through Enos, his generation of people began to call upon God.

After everything was said and done, this was just the beginning of what would grow into a monumental work of God.

Because, when God births a seed in you, that seed will grow.

As time grew on, and nation upon nation of people grew in numbers, soon the world began to take on a dramatic change.

Because when we look at today's society men and women sometimes work the same type of jobs.

Although, we still need to balance the way we were structured to live, we still should not forget where we came from.

From our ancestors of long ago to the reality that the birth of our being had to start from somewhere.

From the dust of the ground to the rib from which she bore, to carry the seeds that will start nations upon nations of people.

The treasure God gave Eve to hold was monumental. Because this seed she spun would birth many nations that would flourish for generations.

And today, it is equally up to men and women to grow this world we live in.

When we think of our ancestors of long ago, we should think of Adam and Eve.

Because this is where it all began, and the rest is History.

About the Author Vera Squire

Vera Squire began writing Poetry and Short Stories at an early age.

Her Short Stories Books are:

Vera Squire 3-Short Stories,

A Short Love Story Called: Socks With Holes In Them,

A Short Christian Play Called:

A Boy and The Calling,

Somebody Is Always Watching,

Somebody Is Always *Watching II*

Somebody Is Always *Watching III*,

Somebody is Always *Watching IV* and Remembering Hurricane Katrina In New Orleans (poetic speaking).

Her mission is to inspire lives.

Be Blessed

This book is the revised version of, A Short Story About Eve, It Was Not An Apple! *(MYSTERY SOLVED)*. (The first edition).

POETRY

MORNING PRAYER

Dress me, God I pray, in the clovers of your splendor,
which arrive like the morning dew.

Even like the dawn,

When it breaks through and peeks into its marvelous
light.

Dress me, God I pray.

From head to toe.

Shape me, and mold me, like the potter shape the clay, from which he makes as he desires.

Dress me, God I pray.

With your wisdom of open collections and place it in my vessel.

Dress me, God I pray,

With your whole armor.

Dress me, God today.

BURDEN BEARER

Come to Him as a little child, casting your cares on the One who bears them all.

Whatever the problem will be,

Jesus says, give them to me.

Full and heavy, these weights I carry,

I wonder, how can I carry more.

I will bring them to my Lord, my Savior Jesus, the One whom I adore.

He said, "My yolk is easy, and burden is light."

I will give them to Him, and He will make it right.

Now to Jesus I will go, and He will heal these blisters and sores.

And He will take these weights I carry, because I can't carry them no more.

JESUS TOUCH

Just one touch, can change the heart that's all that matters.

When praying a prayer so fervently, for the one who is so dear to me, the constant toning of a tone, to the sweet Savior, aroma the room with my faith, I cry for His grace, and His mercy, and His listening ear, to change, and re-arrange this sinner, the one that is so dear.

Because I know, just one touch can change the heart, that's all that matters.

Life

Life spins on a continual dial.

It spins from moments to seconds.

From minutes to hours.

Each movement has power.

And that power belongs to God.

He holds the whole world in the palm of His hand, and He also holds Life.

Love Is

Love is, real

Love is, without Blemish

Love is, Growth

Love is, Forever

Love is, Kind

Love is, Loving

Love is, Loving Yourself

Love is, Loving one another

Love is, Trust

Love is, Complicated

Love is, Free

Love is, Music

Love is, Respect

Love is, Sharing

Love is, Caring

Love is, Priceless

Love is, God and

God is Love

Love is, Pure

Love is, Commitment

Love is, Wholesome

Love is, Worth Loving

Dedication

This book is dedicated to my children, my grandchildren and everyone in my family.

BE BLESSED